Gerardo Hernández Nordelo

Humor from my Pen

Editorial Letra Viva
Coral Gables, La Florida

For more information on the case of the Cuban Five, please contact:

www.freethefive.org
www.thecuban5.org/wordpress/
E-mail: info@freethefive.org
E-mail: info@thecuban5.org

Copyright© 2014 by Editorial *Letra Viva*
251 Valencia Avenue, #253
Coral Gables, La Florida
Design: Nick Sporik
Edition Coordinator: Manuel López
Editorial Board: Alicia Jrapko, Andrés Gómez, Bill Hackwell, Gloria La Riva, Irina Malinovskaya, Lesia Ivashkevich, Manuel López, Nick Sporik.
ALL RIGHTS RESERVED. NO PART OF THIS BOOK MAY BE REPRODUCED IN ANY FORM, EXCEPT FOR THE INCLUSION OF BRIEF QUOTATION IN REVIEW, WITHOUT PERMISSION IN WRITING FROM THE PUBLISHER.
ISBN: 0996107193
ISBN-13: 978-0-9961071-9-8
Printed in the United States of America

CONTENTS

Prologue by Danny Glover	2
Author's Foreword	4
Introduction by Adriana Pérez OConor, author's wife	5
Drawings dedicated to Comandante Fidel Castro	6
Drawings dedicated to the Cuban Revolution	12
Drawings referencing U.S. government policy against Cuba	20
Drawings dedicated to the cause of the Cuban Five	32
About the Cuban Five	38
Message from the Cuban Five to the American People	41
About the Author	44
The story of Cardinal and Gerardo	45
Affidavit of Gerardo Hernández Nordelo	48
Epilogue by Gilbert Brownstone	56

PROLOGUE
by Danny Glover

Gerardo Hernández is my brother in spirit, my brother in purpose and he inspires me, from the first moment that I met him nearly four years ago.

I admire the rest of the five men as well. These men were being proactive in addressing a serious problem that has existed from the beginning of the Cuban Revolution, the relentless attack on the Cuban people. The Cuban Five responded by protecting the Cuban population from U.S.-supported terrorism.

They did this in an honorable way, with the gathering of information, to resolve the situation by presenting this information to the responsible law authorities. For those five men to risk their own lives, in the service of what they believe, to protect their people, is something honorable to me.

I have visited Gerardo many times in Victorville prison. Gerardo in the service of his country never perpetrated any crime to cause his unjust incarceration. Imagine visiting

Danny Glover – American actor. Oscar winner. Doctorate in Art. Glover has performed in more than 70 films and is a U.N. Goodwill Ambassador.

Humor from my Pen

this inhumane place designed as a concentration camp, where they try to kill the spirit. There is no attempt to enhance or rehabilitate the prisoners. If you can imagine this singular man, Gerardo is truly impressive. I remember the visits, seeing him as he waits patiently for the guards to lead him back to the cell, out of reach and the public view of family and friends. Just imagine him standing there, with so much dignity after more than 15 lonely years of this ordeal he has experienced, he is so courageous. He has a tremendous sense of purpose and optimism, a sense of humor and wit that is obvious in his amazing cartoons. Every time I think about him I see him in that moment, in our visit where we are close enough to touch each other. Then he is distant from us, being led away and I always come away feeling that I have to do more. I come away feeling inspired by him and that I've got to do more to free him. I believe we must all work harder to free Gerardo and his brothers.

The love that Gerardo and his wife Adriana have for each other is remarkable, something we would all dream about in a partnership of love. And they have been separated by the U.S. government for more than 15 years. We cannot accept that cruel treatment.

I first became involved with the Cuban Five at the World Social Forum in Brazil, in Porto Alegre in January 2003, almost 11 years ago. I decided that I wanted to join that cause when I looked in the faces of those women, their wives and mothers. That was the key that unlocked the door in my own heart for me.

We need more people to understand the senselessness of what happened, to know what has happened to Cuba for the last 50 plus years. The more that we can bring people to that acknowledgment of who the Five are, the closer we are to the key that will open the door to free our brothers.

Gerardo's mother passed away while he has been incarcerated. We need to internalize that experience, make it ours. Each movement is built around that. The civil rights movement had the same situation, people internalized it, it became our collective experience. It cannot just be the Cuban people who shoulder this burden, we must as well.

Danny Glover

with Saul Landau, filmmaker and journalist

AUTHOR'S FOREWORD

Gerardo Hernández Nordelo

Victorville Federal Prison. California. January 21, 2014.

During the more than 15 years of our unjust imprisonment, the Cuban Five have received many expressions of solidarity from women and men who represent the very best of the American people. Despite the silence, hostility and misinformation that characterizes our case in the mainstream media, there is not a day that passes when we do not receive correspondence from people writing to us for the first time.

It has taken a lot of work but gradually the truth has been emerging and we owe this to the constant efforts of supporters whose contribution to our struggle for justice have been and will remain essential. The Five will always be grateful to that vanguard group of fighters for our freedom, and all people of good will that in one way or another have supported our cause. These remarkable people continue to advocate tirelessly for that day when the entire American people know they have been lied to about our anti-terrorist work in particular and about the reality of Cuba in general.

This book is the result of a "multinational" effort undertaken mainly by comrades in the Ukraine and the United States. To all of them I wish to express my sincere thanks. Most of the cartoons that appear here were motivated by very specific events and in many cases their messages were directed specifically to the Cuban people. Despite that, if American readers can find some meaning in them we would all be satisfied and know that we are advancing.

INTRODUCTION
by Adriana Pérez OConor, author's wife

I am not telling the story of a movie. I am talking about real life. More than 25 years ago I married Gerardo. We had hoped, like any other young couple, to create a family with at least two children. We had many plans, and I could not have imagined this reality that I have lived during these past 15 years, a home without Gerardo, without the children we planned.

However, consecutive U.S. administrations are responsible for the situation which we five Cuban families are living. It is the U.S. government's cruel and hostile policy that led Gerardo, Ramón, Antonio, René and Fernando to fight against terrorism. If that were not the case, we would not have had to be separated nor suffered so greatly. These are men who sacrificed their youth and even risked their lives to defend all of us in Cuba.

It has been more than 15 years of an exhausting legal process, more than 15 years of constant struggle, of psychological torture, more than 15 years of waking up each morning without a kiss or embrace from Gerardo. It has been 15 years, dreaming of a better future.

Every day, from the moment I awake, I ask myself thousands of questions. But there is one question that has never changed in all these years. When will this nightmare end? President Obama has the answer to my question. He is a man who is a lawyer, who has a beautiful family, who wakes up each day by his wife's side, and who received the Nobel Peace Prize. In reality only he can end this nightmare. That is why I ask Obama time and again not to carry this responsibility on his shoulders of holding Gerardo, Ramón, Antonio and Fernando prisoner. Obama is not responsible for the unjust arrest and conviction of the Cuban Five, but he is responsible for not providing at least a humanitarian solution to this case. Obama can change our reality today. That is why I tell him, "Mr. President, do it today; tomorrow will be too late." Regardless of what happens, I will be here, because the best thing I have done in my life was to marry Gerardo. And the best thing I will continue to do in my life is struggle to see him return.

Adriana Pérez OConor, the wife of Gerardo Hernández, spoke in Toronto at the event, "Breaking the Silence: Justice for the Five, People's Tribunal and Assembly," which took place on September 21-23, 2012.

Humor from my Pen

Happy Birthday, Comandante!
Lompoc Federal Prison, California, August 13, 2002

Humor from my Pen

7

¡Felicidades Comandante!

H. Nordelo 05

PRISIÓN DE VICTORVILLE, AGOSTO 13.

Happy Birthday, Comandante!
Victorville Prison, August 13, 2005

Humor from my Pen

- ...Watch out! He might have a different number, but he's still the most powerful batter...

Happy Birthday, Comandante!

Victorville Prison, 2006, California

Humor from my Pen

Happy Birthday, Fidel!!!

Victorville Prison, California, August, 2007

Other weapons, same struggle...
Congratulations Comandante, on your 82nd birthday!
Victorville Prison, California, August, 2008

Humor from my Pen

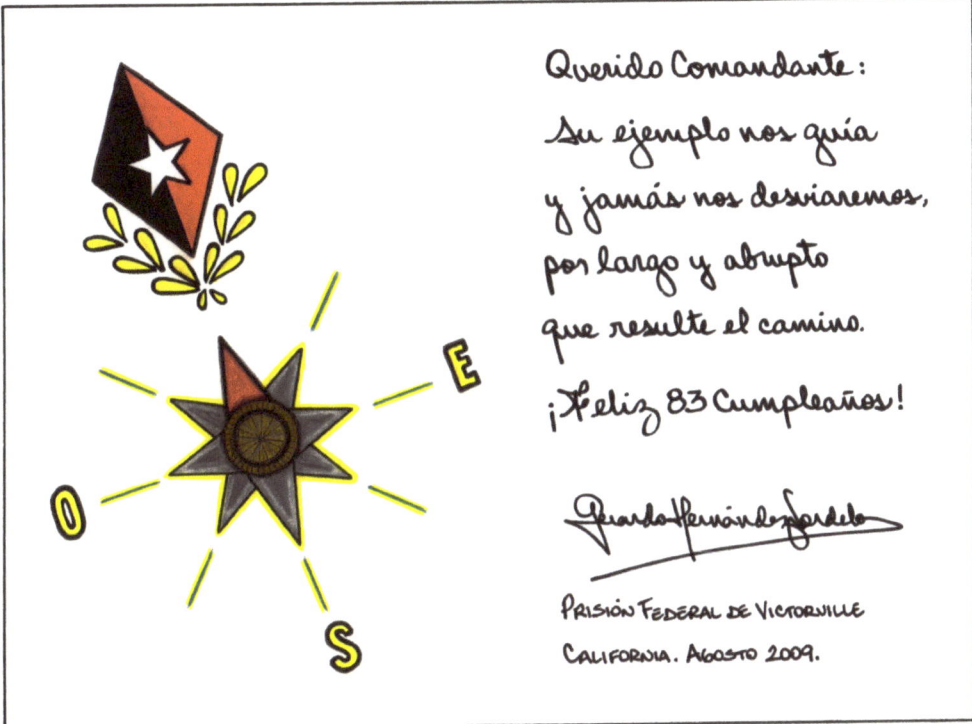

Dear Comandante!
Your example guides us and we will never go astray, no matter how long and arduous the journey is!

Happy 83rd birthday!

Victorville Federal Prison, California, August, 2009

Humor from my Pen

Queridos hermanos:

Celebramos con ustedes el 46 Aniversario de nuestra Revolución, con el creciente orgullo de pertenecer a un pueblo aguerrido, al que ninguna amenaza podrá jamás intimidar. Nos inspira el legado de los héroes y mártires de la patria, a quienes debemos honrar eternamente, y nos alienta el ejemplo de dignidad y resistencia de todos ustedes. ¡Felicidades compañeros!
¡Que el 2005 sea, con el esfuerzo de todos, un año de nuevas victorias, y de avances en la realización de nuestros sueños!
¡Gracias una vez más, por su importante solidaridad!

Con el abrazo revolucionario
y fidelista de los cinco:

Prisión Federal de Victorville, Diciembre 2004.

Dear brothers and sisters!
We are celebrating the 46th anniversary of our Revolution, with the ever-increasing pride of belonging to a combative people that no kind of threat could ever weaken. We are inspired by the legacy of our heroes and national martyrs, which we will forever honor, and we are encouraged by the example of dignity and resistance that all of you provide.
Congratulations, comrades!
Let's direct our common efforts to make the year 2005 a year of new victories and progress in the fulfillment of our common dreams.
Once more, thank you for your important solidarity!
Revolutionary greetings and a Fidelista embrace, from the Five.
Victorville Federal Prison, December, 2004

Lyrics (top): "... a sharpened machete awaits them"
(Bubble): I love the sound of any explosion in Cuba, except for an explosion of joy; that I really can't stand...
Congratulations, brothers! Onward!
Victorville Federal Prison, California, December, 2005

- He said that this New Year would be the year he would eat us in Havana...
- He who lives with illusions today, dies of disappointment tomorrow!
Congratulations, brothers and sisters, on the 48th anniversary of the Revolution! Let's make 2007 yet another year of struggle and of victories! A Fidelista embrace from the Five, for all of you.
Victorville Prison, December, 2006

OUR OWN FORMULA
Brothers and sisters, congratulations on the 49th anniversary
(of the Revolution)! Let's keep working to perfect this great project that
has meant so much sacrifice, that others dream of destroying.
Thank you for making us feel so proud to be revolutionary Cubans.
A Fidelista embrace, from the Five.
Victorville Prison, California, December, 2007

- Fifty! It's about time for them to get a clue...
- ... that here we are absolutely fearless and totally unshakeable!
Congratulations to all the Cubans and our brothers and sisters worldwide, who through their solidarity have made this great Revolution their own!
Victorville Federal Prison, California, December, 2008

Humor from my Pen

Here, have another one!
(On the bull): Media war, mercenaries, blockade, hate, terrorism, etc...
Congratulations, brothers and sisters!

Victorville Prison, December, 2009

The "oil" we most need to find:

Efficiency, productivity, organization, quality, discipline, responsibility, economy, constancy, a demanding nature

Congratulations, brothers, on the 54th anniversary of the Revolution!

Humor from my Pen

Editor's note: This picture was drawn by Gerardo Hernández Nordelo for the "Heberprot-P Havana 2012" Congress, which took place on December 10-11, 2012 in Cuba's capital. The drawing depicts a competition between the medicine "Heberprot-P" and a hacksaw, symbolizing the amputation that threatens many diabetic patients with foot ulcers. The Cuban medicine easily wins the competition – proving the general recognition achieved by Heberprot-B in the treatment of such ulcers.

Humor from my Pen

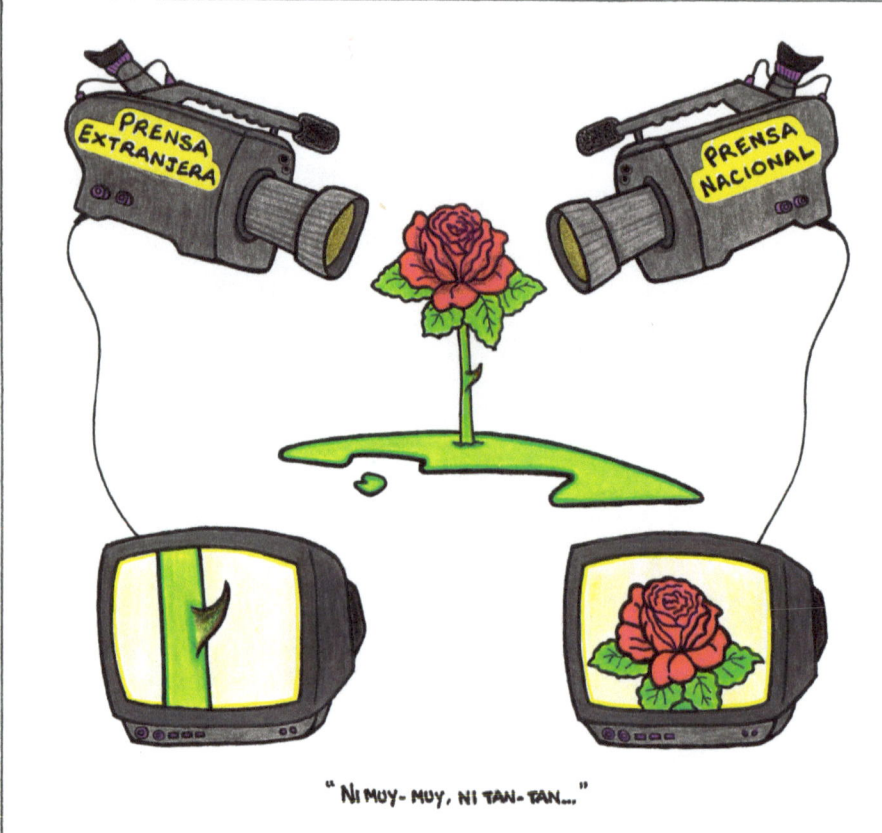

FOREIGN PRESS   **CUBAN PRESS**

"Neither so bad nor so good..."
We wish all Cuban journalists great success on the occasion of their 8th Congress, and in the necessary efforts ahead to ensure that Cubans can rely on a media that is ever more revolutionary in the battle to perfect our socialism.
A strong embrace from the Five.
Victorville Prison, California, July, 2008

Humor from my Pen

We'll fight terrorists anywhere in the world...

Humor from my Pen

The two faces of Mr. Bush:
(in Washington) - The terrorists are evil, immoral murderers...
(in Miami) - ... but if they can decide the vote in elections, they are "poor exiles and freedom fighters..."

The Miami mafia throws a banquet in honor of the President...
- ... And I promise you that Cuba will be free!
- (Make sure he doesn't drink any more "Cuba libres")

Of course Cuba hurts!

26 Humor from my Pen

- For some "high-ranking" U.S. politicians, the previous "Chairman" of the so-called "Cuban"-American National Foundation was a $aint...
- ... and the new one is $uper $aintly!

Only in Miami!

Posada in Miami
Editor's note: The author refers to the terrorist Luis "Posada" Carriles. In Spanish "Posada" is the participle of the verb "posarse" – "to alight" (in regard to birds).

Humor from my Pen

BIN LADEN'S NEW VIDEO

- I am announcing my anti-discrimination lawsuit against the mainstream media ...

- ...I demand that they refer to me as an "activist," "freedom fighter," and "legendary militant"

-...just like they always do with the anti-Cuban terrorists!

Humor from my Pen

Humor from my Pen

A letter written by Gerardo Hernandez Nordelo explaining how he produced the logo which identifies the fight to free the Cuban Five:

The logo was created in August, 2002 at the request of comrade Alicia Jrapko, a member of the U.S. National Committee to Free the Cuban Five.

The Committee planned to hold a demonstration, and Alicia contacted me and asked me to provide her a picture to be placed on posters and banners.

All I had at my disposal were a few colored markers and a scrap of postcard.

For obvious reasons, I opted for the figure 5 as a basis for a logo, and included our Cuban flag which was essential in the picture.

Some months later, with great honor and satisfaction we accepted the titles of Heroes of the Republic of Cuba and from that point onward a gold star appeared on the logo (though on some websites one can see a red star).

In one of the first messages sent by us to our people we mentioned "a sea of flags" of which we are so proud when we watch the Cuban demonstrations and forums on some news broadcasts. As a result, the lower part of the figure 5 on the logo represents a wave in this sea of flags.

As I had no tools for drawing, I used a tin cap to draw an internal circle and a plastic glass for the external one.

At the time, due to some incidents in the prison, convicts were locked in solitary, each in his cell. So when I finished the first sketch, I did not have anyone to show it to and ask for an opinion. I called a Mexican from the next cell over, and asked him to reach outside the bars with a mirror. In my turn, I stretched my drawing, so that he could see it. I asked the Mexican if he liked my picture of the number 5, and he said "yes". Later, I learned that he had been sleeping and I woke him up. So, I understood that if I had asked him whether he liked my sketch of the number 8, he would also have answered "yes."

Recently among other papers I found my first sketch of a logo drawn with a pencil and sent it to my wife Adriana.

Alicia and Bill have the original with all its original colors.

It's a great honor for me that my four brothers liked the logo, and that it is used not only in the Cuban mass media, but also by a number of the solidarity committees all over the world which are fighting for our release.

Humor from my Pen

WITH LOVE AND HUMOR, EVERYTHING IS POSSIBLE
Editor's note: Picture drawn by Gerardo Hernández Nordelo for the cover of his book of drawings "You Can Achieve Everything with Love and Humor," published in Cuba in 2002.

Humor from my Pen

Editor's note: The logo drawn by Gerardo Hernández Nordelo for the concert "Five stars and one song," held at the Theatre of the Hostos Center for Arts & Culture in New York, USA on September 14, 2008

Editor's note: The logo drawn by Gerardo Hernández Nordelo for the "La Joven Cuba" blog (Cuba's Young), created on initiative of the students, young lecturers and scientists at the National University of Matanzas, Cuba.

Editor's note: The logo was designed by Gerardo Hernández Nordelo to accompany all his cartoons drawn in prison. Gerardo's exhibit "Humor from my Pen" was shown for the first time at SPARC Gallery in Venice, California, USA on June 4, 2011.

Humor from my Pen 35

Acudo en este día a tu nombre, en este día de singular verano, aquel lejano, si estoy tan firme, padre, no te asombres. No soy aquel niño, pero hoy soy el hombre que tus sueños llevaba de la mano, a mi firmeza pongo tu nombre, para limpio y pleno, ampuloso, amatorio...

I came to your life that day, that unique, strict, resolute, bright, faraway summer day. Father, don't wonder, that I am so firm. I'm not the same, but today I am a man, who your dreams took by the hand, I am not a child, but standing clean and wholesome, my strength is yours entirely.

Editor's note: This picture was drawn by Gerardo Hernández Nordelo for the book of poetry by Antonio Guerrero Rodríguez "Truth calls me," presented at the 12th International Book Fair in Cuba, 2013.

Humor from my Pen

Editor's note: Additional drawings by Gerardo Hernández Nordelo for Antonio Guerrero Rodríguez's book of poetry "Truth calls me," presented at the 12th International Book Fair in Cuba, 2013.

Humor from my Pen

In memory of Ahmed. We share in the sorrow of his family and friends.

<u>Editor's note:</u> **Ahmed Velásquez Sagués was a great Cuban press photographer for "Granma" newspaper. He died of a heart attack on December 29, 2004 at the age of 39.**

ABOUT THE CUBAN FIVE

Since 1998 five Cuban citizens, known internationally as the Cuban Five, have been subjected to numerous and grave violations of their fundamental rights by the U.S. government. Their names are Gerardo Hernández Nordelo, Ramón Labañino Salazar, Antonio Guerrero Rodríguez, Fernando González Llort and René González Sehwerert.

These men were arrested on September 12, 1998 by the FBI, convicted in a Miami court in 2001 and sentenced to terms ranging from 15 years to life, including two life sentences for Gerardo Hernández. They were falsely charged and wrongly convicted of conspiracy to commit espionage and related charges.

The Cuban Five never conspired to commit espionage. They were on a mission to monitor and report to their government on terrorist Cuban American organizations in Miami that are well known by the U.S. government to be responsible for terrorist attacks against the Cuban people.

These terrorist organizations based in Miami and their violent actions against the Cuban people are the result of an active policy of the U.S. government of state terrorism against Cuba since 1959. It was the U.S. government that originally recruited, trained, financed and directed these extreme right-wing Cuban American terrorists and that today offer them protection from their actions, allowing them to act with impunity.

Their five decade long campaign of sabotage, bombings, assassinations and other attacks has left 3,478 Cubans dead and 2,099 seriously and permanently injured. Moreover, because of this terror campaign, the Cuban economy has suffered economic losses of more than $54 billion dollars.

The Cuban Five were peacefully trying to do what U.S. law enforcement authorities have refused to do: prevent terrorism. With their work they prevented violent actions in Cuba and thus saved the lives and well-being of countless innocent Cubans, especially children, women and the elderly.

Two of the Five have returned to Cuba. René González Sehwerert and Fernando González Llort, after serving their full sentences of 15 and 17 years, respectively, were released from prison and are now in Cuba with their families, where they are active participants in the worldwide effort to gain the immediate release of their three brothers who remain imprisoned.

Gerardo Hernández Nordelo, the author of the works in this book, was convicted to two life sentences plus 15 additional years in prison. He was falsely charged by the U.S.

government. The maliciousness of U.S. authorities against Gerardo can be explained by the fact that they have stated that Gerardo was the leader of the group.

Since the arrest of the Cuban Five, more than fifteen years ago, Gerardo Hernández has been imprisoned in maximum security prisons with all the restrictions and abuses that such facilities imply. Moreover, for all these years his wife, Adriana Pérez OConor, has been denied U.S. visas to enter the United States in order to visit her husband.

An ever growing network of committees, 300 strong, is currently organized in at least 100 countries throughout the world to demand the immediate release from jail of the Cuban Five. In the U.S. there are two networks composed of more than 30 committees and countless individuals also demanding their immediate release from prison.

In August, 2005, a three-judge panel from the 11th Circuit Court of Appeals unanimously ruled to overturn the men's convictions, but the Bush administration successfully moved to overturn this decision.

Numerous human rights organizations and leading international figures have also demanded the immediate release of the Cuban Five given the nature of their work in the U.S. and their arbitrary arrests, trial and convictions in Miami.

These include the U.N. Working Group on Arbitrary Detentions; Amnesty International; 10 Nobel Prize recipients: Adolfo Pérez Esquivel, Rigoberta Menchú, Günter Grass, José Ramos-Horta, Wole Soyinka, Nadine Gordiner, José Saramago, Zhores Alferov, Darío Fo, Máiread Corrigan Maguire; and also, Miguel D'Escoto, Ramsey Clark, Noam Chomsky, Alice Walker and president Jimmy Carter. Freedom for the Cuban Five has also been called for by famous actors Danny Glover, Edward Asner, Susan Sarandon, Oliver Stone, Martin Sheen, Pete Seeger, Ry Cooder and many others.

The policies of successive U.S. administrations in place for more than half a century against the fundamental rights of the Cuban people to independence and self determination would explain U.S. vindictiveness against the Cuban Five.

We demand the immediate release of three of the Cuban Five who remain unjustly imprisoned in the United States!

Gerardo Hernández Nordelo

Born in Havana on June 4, 1965. A graduate of the Higher Institute of International Relations Raúl Roa García, Cuba, 1989. Degree in international relations. Artist cartoonist. During his entire prison term, his wife, Adriana Pérez OConor has been denied a visa to visit him. Sentenced to two life terms in prison plus 15 years.
Hero of the Republic of Cuba.

Ramón Labañino Salazar

Born in Havana on June 9, 1963. A graduate of the University of Havana with honors, Cuba, 1986. Economist. Athlete. Poet. Has three daughters. Sentenced to 30-year imprisonment. Hero of the Republic of Cuba.

Antonio Guerrero Rodríguez

Born in Miami on October 16, 1958. Graduate of the Kiev Institute of Civil Aviation (now National Aviation University), Ukraine, 1983. Airport construction engineer. Poet. Painter. Athlete. Has two sons. Sentenced to 22-year imprisonment.
Hero of the Republic of Cuba.

Fernando González Llort

Born in Havana on August 18, 1963. A graduate of the Higher Institute of International Relations Raúl Roa García, with honors, Cuba, 1987. Degree in international relations. Sentenced to 17-year imprisonment. Returned to Cuba on February 28, 2014, after serving full sentence. Hero of the Republic of Cuba.

Rene González Sehwerert

Born in Chicago on August 13, 1956. A graduate of the School of Aviation Carlos Ulloa, Cuba. Pilot instructor. Writer. Has two daughters. All throughout his prison sentence he was forbidden to meet with his wife Olga Salanueva. Served entire 15-year prison sentence plus additional punishment of probation. Released from prison on October 7, 2011. In April 2013 he was allowed to return to his homeland (Cuba), subject to rejection of his U.S. citizenship. Hero of the Republic of Cuba.

Message from THE CUBAN FIVE to the American people

We are five loyal Cubans, who for 33 months and five days have endured a severe imprisonment in the jails of a nation, where hostility against our own is obvious with its authorities. After a long and infamous trial directed by manifestly political objectives, methods and procedures and overwhelmed by a real deluge of maliciously concocted propaganda, we have decided to address the American people to let them know the truth, that we are the victims of a terrible injustice.

We have been accused of endangering the security of the United States and indicted on numerous charges, including crimes such as conspiracy to commit murder; charges that could not, and cannot, be proven, for they are false, but for which we could be sentenced to dozens of years of imprisonment and even to life sentences.

A body of Miami jurors, and this explains it all, declared us guilty of all charges. But we are simply Cuban patriots and it was never our intention to cause any harm, either to the values or the integrity of the American people.

Our tiny nation, that has heroically survived four decades of aggressions and threats to its national security, along with subversive plots, sabotage and destabilization, has every right to defend itself from its enemies who keep using the U.S. territory to plan, organize and finance terrorist actions, breaking your own laws in the process.

Our country is also entitled to peace, respect for its sovereignty and for our most sacred interests.

In the four years that we have spent in this country, we have never stopped wondering why it is that our two peoples cannot live in peace and how it is possible that the vicious interests of the extreme right-wing, including terrorist groups and organizations made up of Cuban Americans, can strain relations between two peoples who are so close geographically and could easily maintain relations based on respect and equality.

While in prison, we have had time to reflect on our behavior in this country and we can say, without the shadow of a doubt, that neither with our attitude nor our actions have we in any way interfered with, or jeopardized the security of, the American people. What we have certainly done is contribute to exposing terrorist plots and actions against our people, thus preventing the death of innocent Cubans and Americans.

Why is it necessary for Cuban patriots to be kept away from their loved ones and postpone an otherwise joyful life with their families and people, for having performed the honorable duty of protecting their homeland?

Why are the U.S. authorities tolerant with these terrorists who act against our country? Why don't they investigate or take action against the terrorist plots denounced by Cuba or try to prevent the numerous attempts against the life of our leaders?

Why is it that the professed authors of these and other terrorist actions are still loose in South Florida, as was clearly established during the trial?

Who trained them and who allows them to carry out their plans?

Who are those really endangering the security of the United States of America?

They are the terrorist groups made up of Cuban Americans and their political and economic mentors in America who are gnawing away at the credibility of this country, giving this nation an appearance of ruthlessness and misleading its institutions to an inconsistent, prejudiced and erratic behavior. They are the same individuals who forestall a serious and sensitive approach to Cuba related issues.

Such groups and their mentors have joined in a coordinated drive to bring about conflict between our two countries. To that end, they keep promoting with both the legislative and the executive branches of government increasingly aggressive measures against Cuba.

They want to continue to foment a long-standing history of invasions, sabotage, biological aggressions and other similar actions, while sparing no effort to create situations that might lead to incidents of grave consequence to both our peoples.

The result of such aggressions against Cuba is that 3,478 people were killed and 2,099 have been maimed between 1959 and 1999, not to mention very costly material losses.

Yet, they persist in their propaganda campaigns, offering the American people a distorted image of Cuba, and using various pretexts, trying to block laws and

Humor from my Pen

regulations that would allow Americans to travel freely to Cuba to know firsthand the real situation there. Likewise, they set every obstacle to cooperation in areas of common interest such as illegal migration and the drug-trafficking that brings so much pain to the American people.

All this is compounded by constant requests for new and ever increasing budgets from the government, thus affecting the American taxpayers, simply to finance their actions against Cuba. The enormous amounts of money that keep pouring into radio and TV broadcasts, as well as to financing their projects on the island, take away resources that could better be used to cope with social problems afflicting Americans.

The examples of these groups' clout and pressures on the Miami community, its government agencies and even its judicial system, continue to the present day.

It would be in the best interest of the American people to put an end to the negative influence of such extremists and terrorists that cause so much damage to the United States by breaking its own laws.

We have never done anything for money. We have always lived modestly and acted humbly, living up to the sacrifices of our own people.

We have always been moved by a strong sentiment of human solidarity, love for our homeland and contempt for that which contradicts the dignity of human beings.

The defendants in this trial are in no way repentant of what we have done to defend our country. We declare ourselves not guilty and simply take comfort in the fact that we have honored our duty to our people and our homeland. Our loved ones understand the profound nature of the ideas that guide us and take pride in our sacrifices for humanity in this struggle against terrorism and for the independence of Cuba.

René González   Antonio Guerrero   Fernando González   Gerardo Hernández   Ramón Labañino

June 17, 2001

ABOUT THE AUTHOR

The author of the drawings is Gerardo Hernández Nordelo, a talented person and versatile personality, awarded with the title of the Hero of the Republic of Cuba. He was born in Havana on June 4th, 1965. Since childhood, Gerardo grew up as a sociable, active and cheerful boy. He took an active part in his school life.

In 1989 he graduated from the University of International Relations in Havana. As a student, Gerardo showed excellent results. During his student years he began drawing cartoons, as well as performing in the "Aspirin" theater company. Gerardo's humorous stories, with the main character being Pepino, a cucumber, were often published in newspapers and magazines in Cuba.

In 1988, he met Adriana Pérez OConor, who became his faithful wife.

In 1989 Gerardo performed an internationalist mission in Angola, for which he was awarded with two medals, one as an "Internationalist Warrior" and the other "For Friendship Between Cuba and the People's Republic of Angola."

In the mid-1990s, Gerardo became a member of the anti-terrorist group working in the United States, whose mission was to provide information in order to prevent terrorist attacks against Cuba, which, at the time, were being actively prepared by radical organizations of ultra right-wing Cuban exiles from Miami. Thanks to Gerardo and his four companions, Antonio Guerrero, Fernando Gonzalez, Ramón Labañino and René Gonzalez, more than 170 terrorist attacks against the people of Cuba were averted, saving hundreds of people at the very least. However, the U.S. authorities took no interest in stopping terrorist attacks against the Republic of Cuba, and on September 12th, 1998, Gerardo and his four comrades were arrested, subjected to an unfair trial and sentenced to severe prison terms. Gerardo received two life terms in prison plus 15 years.

For his homeland and relatives, Gerardo's arrest was a huge shock. The unjust trial against the "Cuban Five", as Gerardo, Ramón, Antonio, Fernando and René became known worldwide, sparked outrage and protests across the globe and became a prime exhibit in the U.S. government's claimed campaign against terrorism. The movement to free the Cuban Five encompassed all continents, the United States first and foremost.

Even imprisoned, Gerardo and his associates show their strength and will.

From prison, Gerardo produces his clever and talented sketches devoted to political and universal issues, some of which are found in this book.

The story of CARDINAL and GERARDO

Once upon a time, a bird made friends with a prisoner. Both were incarcerated in the United States and both were unjustly imprisoned for defending Cuba from terrorist activity.

This is how the story began. On June 4, 2009, the same day as his birthday, Gerardo Hernández heard about this creature. He found out about it through a prisoner whose last name was Lira, who worked in the prison factory. Lira and a guard were cleaning the roof with a pressure hose and without meaning to or perhaps without knowing, they destroyed a nest that contained three chicks. Two of them died instantly but one remained alive. They were so tiny that they didn't even have any feathers. It's possible that they had just barely hatched.

The guard was visibly moved, and feeling responsible, allowed Lira to bring the chick secretly inside the prison to try to save it. The prisoner arrived with the chick in the palm of his hand and not knowing what to do with it, began to ask the other prisoners what to do. Someone suggested: "Ask Cuba [the nickname the prisoners had given Gerardo]; he likes animals and surely he will know what to do." That's how Gerardo came to be summoned, and he came to the cell where they kept the bird.

Gerardo's first reaction was to whistle, imitating what he imagined the chick's mother would have done. He moved his fingers as though they were little wings. Miraculously, the little bird opened its beak. Gerardo began to give it breadcrumbs and later, dipped his fingers in water and let the drops fall softly into the little bird's beak.

Gerardo didn't want to take the bird to his cell, but every day he went to feed it. The problem was that at the beginning, the bird didn't want to take food from anyone except Gerardo. One day it occurred to Gerardo to offer the chick a few slivers of fish, and afterwards the rascal didn't want breadcrumbs any more. His feathers began to grow and so Gerardo taught it to eat on its own. He put the bits of food in the palm of his hand and the little bird came fearlessly.

Humor from my Pen

However, the prisoners were worried. If an inspection were to happen, the little bird would be a problem. Since he was already quite a bit bigger, they let him loose in the patio so that he might fly free. The bird flew a little while and then returned to Gerardo's shoulder. Every time he tried to fly with the other birds, they rejected him with little pecks. Little by little he gained confidence. Gerardo went alone to the wing where his cell was, but when he returned to the patio, the bird also returned to see him.

Once there were many prisoners in the patio. Someone told Gerardo that the bird was perched on the concertina wire surrounding the prison. Gerardo whistled, and in front of all the prisoners, the little bird appeared out of nowhere and landed on his shoulder. Incredible. Everyone talked about it.

The little bird was named Cardinal, because Gerardo had painted its tailfeathers with a red marker to distinguish him from all the rest. The ink affected the bird a bit. It lost its tail feathers but only for a little while. Later they grew back, in their natural color. However, the name remained: Cardinal.

On a different occasion another prisoner found the little bird in the patio with its beak stretched open. It was very hot, and the bird was thirsty. Gerardo gave it water. He hid the bird under his hat in order to go inside without the bird being seen. Of course the guards realized he had something odd on his head. "What's under the hat?" they asked, and Gerardo answered, "Nothing." Cardinal answered as well, whistling like crazy. "Don't tell me you're training him to take messages to Fidel," said one of the guards, laughing.

The story didn't end there. Gerardo brought the bird to his cell and made a nest for him to stay there with him. He played with him, letting him rest on his shoulder, or on his head. When Gerardo was writing, the bird came to play and Gerardo would pet him gently, to calm him. So Cardinal would run along his back, where he'd be out of reach. Sometimes he curled up inside Gerardo's collar and slept there. Or he pecked at his friend's ear and when Gerardo moved his head, he'd go for the other ear.

Once when Gerardo had let Cardinal go, he flew toward the cafeteria and landed on the plate of a very large, tough prisoner who was eating a piece of chicken. The prisoner caught the bird in his hands, meaning to strangle him and someone shouted, "Don't kill him! He belongs to Cuba." The outcry took the prisoner by surprise. He let Cardinal go and asked, surprised, "And who the hell is Cuba?"

Gerardo was actually very worried. A certain guard was not showing any mercy toward the little bird. During an inspection, the guard had forced Gerardo to let Cardinal go, and closed the door behind him. The little bird returned later, completely exhausted. Gerardo let him rest for a few days inside his cell. And then came the lockdown (solitary confinement as punishment for all prisoners), and whenever there's a lockdown, there are inspections.

When Gerardo heard that they were checking all the space between the floor and the door, he pushed Cardinal outside. Cardinal flew, within the wing where Gerardo's cell was located. When

Humor from my Pen

the guard arrived, he saw the box where Cardinal lived. Gerardo said that this was where his friend lived, of his own free will: "The problem is that I take him outside and he returns; it's not my fault." "Look," said the guard, gesturing as though to say he thought Gerardo was nuts, "if you think I'm going to believe that bird is going to return..."

Gerardo whistled from his cell and the guard froze in his tracks as he watched the bird return. Cardinal had no problem picking out the cell belonging to his friend, among the huge array of cells on two floors that looked exactly alike.

Cardinal arrived at Gerardo's cell. He looked at him through the bars but couldn't enter (since this was lockdown). He waited there nervously, until Gerardo couldn't stand it any more and opened the slot where food was delivered, and Cardinal came in. A few days later there was another inspection. When the guards arrived at Gerardo's cell, he told them that he had a small bird, so they wouldn't be scared if the bird should happen to fly overhead. He was told that he had to release it, but since none of them could catch the bird, they brought Gerardo to the entrance for the entire wing so that he could let it go himself.

Since they were in lockdown, Gerardo and the little bird walked down the passageway, escorted by the guards. All the other prisoners saw them through the bars of their cells and began to shout: "They're taking Cuba and the bird to the hole!" as they banged their doors in protest. The guard shouted, "Calm down! He's not going to the hole; we're just going to free the bird!"

That was the last time that Gerardo saw Cardinal. The lockdown lasted a month while the wing was completely shut down. Gerardo couldn't leave and Cardinal couldn't enter. The little bird had been inside this rough high-security prison since Gerardo's birthday, from June 4th, and he remained there until July 16th, one day after the wedding anniversary of Gerardo and his wife, Adriana.

And that's the end of this (true) story.

Alicia Jrapko

Editor's note: Alicia Jrapko and Bill Hackwel are the coordinators of the International Committee for the Freedom of the Cuban Five. Alicia wrote this story from memory, two hours after hearing it from Gerardo during a visit to the maximum security prison in Victorville, California. Gerardo later revised and corrected the text. This article was published for the first time on Cubadebate, in November 17, 2009.

AFFIDAVIT of Gerardo Hernández Nordelo

UNITED STATES DISTRICT COURT
SOUTHERN DISTRICT OF FLORIDA
CASE NO. 10-21957-Civ-LENARD
Criminal Case No. 98-721-Cr-LENARD
GERARDO HERNANDEZ,
Movant,
AFFIDAVIT of Gerardo Hernández
v.
UNITED STATES,
Respondent_____

I, Gerardo Hernández, declare under penalty of perjury as follows:

1. I am the above-named Movant and make this affidavit in support of the motion to vacate, set aside or correct judgement and sentence under 28 U.S.C. 2255, filed on June 14, 2010.

2. At trial I was represented by Paul A. McKenna, a court appointed attorney practicing in Miami, Florida. I had not previously met him. I can't recall if Mr. McKenna and I ever had a conversation prior to trial about severance.

3. What I do recall is that he never explained to me that it would be possible to have a separate trial on Count III at which time I would have the right to testify on my own behalf on the conspiracy to murder charge free of the prejudice to other charges, and to my co-defendants. Had I known that, I would have insisted on exercising my right to testify in my defense in the conspiracy to murder trial to show how wrong the prosecution's interpretations of its evidence were, and provide the jury with the truth.

4. Nor did Mr. McKenna explain to me that at a separate trial, I could secure the testimony of one or more of my co-defendants without their having to choose between incriminating themselves or refusing to give relevant evidence at my trial on the conspiracy to murder charge.

5. What I never understood, because it was never explained to me until now, that under United States law, I could have requested a separate trial on the conspiracy to murder charge alone in order to testify and present evidence pertinent to that count. I had no prior experience in the US court system and was unaware that a severance

with his mom Carmen Nordelo

Humor from my Pen

with his niece Yadira

would have allowed for such presentation. Had I known that, I would have insisted that my lawyer make every effort to secure a separate trial on that count. If Count III were severed and separately tried I would have testified to establish my innocence.

6. Had I known that I could have had a separate trial on Count III, I would have testified at my trial on that count, in essence, as follows:

A. Prior to the events of February 24, 1996, and up to the present time, I knew and know nothing about any alleged plan to shoot down aircraft of the Brothers to the Rescue.

B. None of the actions that I did take in advance of February 24th, 1996, were intended to be part of any such alleged plan, nor was I aware that any of my actions would contribute to any such alleged plan, if it existed.

C. As I knew nothing about any alleged plan to shoot down any aircraft, still less did I intend to contribute to or have any knowledge of, any alleged plan that would cause any aircraft to be shot down in international airspace or in the territorial and maritime jurisdiction of the United States, as alleged in Count III of the indictment.

D. During the time I was on vacation in Cuba from early November 1995 until my return to Miami on the 26th of January, 1996, I received no information from any source about any alleged plan to shoot down aircraft nor any attempt to threaten, warn or militarily confront them but I did know from public statements by the Cuban Government that it would not tolerate new violations of the Cuban sovereignty by BTTR aircrafts, as those which took place on January 9th and 13th, 1996.

E. I would testify that any reference or notation I might have made on a budgetary report that I had received funds "at Headquarters" or "MX" should not be read, as suggested by the Government, that I was ever present at a meeting at the

with his sister Chabela and his nephew Alier

Humor from my Pen

with Leonard Weinglass, U.S. lawyer

command center.

F. I would have explained to the jury that because I was a covert agent, I was strictly prohibited from entering any establishment connected to the clandestine services, as that could reveal my real job and jeopardize my mission. This was true, even in Cuba, where we knew the United States had counter-intelligence agents.

G. I would have also testified that I was instructed about a plan entitled "Operation Venecia" which was designed to "neutralize the counterrevolutionary actions of BTTR," developed by the Directorate of Intelligence in early December of 1995. See Appendix B attached to the 2255 Memorandum. Its purpose was to "call attention of the national and international public opinion" to the activities of BTTR in violating Cuban sovereignty and international law by having German (Roque) return to Cuba and make a public denunciation of BTTR.

H. I was instructed to work on assuring his return "at the end of February or beginning of March 1996."

I. I would have explained that at no time ever, neither during my stay in Cuba nor before, nor after it, was there any mention of any plan to shoot down BTTR aircraft anywhere nor any other form of communication that led me to believe or suspect the existence of such a plan.

At no time did anyone express to me any concern about the activities of BTTR while flying in international airspace. However, there was concern about BTTR's public announcements that it intended to continue to conduct operations in Cuban airspace in violation of Cuban sovereignty.

J. Had I been given an opportunity to testify, I would have explained to the jury that during my months away from Miami, my work was taken over by another agent, A-4 (known to me only as A-4 or Miguel. I do not know his actual name.). He moved into my apartment in North Miami and I gave him my decoding disk which was imprinted with a program that permitted the user to decode messages to and from Cuba.

We each had our own laptops. I took mine with me when I returned

with Martin Garbus, U.S. lawyer

Humor from my Pen

Gloria La Riva, coordinator of the National Committee to Free the Cuban 5

to Cuba. While these laptops, standing alone, could not send and receive messages, they had the capacity to turn a series of numbers that had been received on a high frequency radio and fed into them, into a coherent message, but only with the aid of a floppy disk that contained a decoding program. There was just a single floppy disk in the apartment and I left it with A-4 when I went on vacation.

K. When I returned to my apartment in North Miami, toward the end of January, 1996, A-4 remained and continued to use the decoding disk. As a Major, he outranked me since I was only a lieutenant. For the several months before he left, he had the disk and was sending and receiving messages. The messages were sent in a code that was common to both of us but only A-4 had the capability to decode the messages through the use of the disk at that time. Although I had access to the disk it remained principally in his possession. It wasn't until early March 1996 that A-4 was directed to turn over the decoding program to me.

L. I do not recall ever receiving a message referencing Operation Escorpion. Given the opportunity, I would have testified that I did not write or send the message of February 12, 1996 which was labelled DG104 at trial and which was directed to "Iselin" advising that no agent should fly on BTTR aircraft during the weekend of February 24-27, 1996. I never referred to that agent by that name, but rather used his other code name, "Castor", as shown by many other reports in the evidence. (During the trial the Government contended that "Castor" was Rene Gonzalez). I do not know why my name was added to that document as a signatory. Among the hundreds of reports that were part of the seized documentary materials, this one, to the best of my recollection, was the only one allegedly signed by two officers.

M. I would have wanted to tell the jury that given what I did know about

with Father Michael Lapsley, South African priest

with Father Geoff Bottoms, english priest

the long history of provocations by BTTR, and how they had been responded to date, any deliberate confrontation outside Cuban territorial airspace was simply something I could not have imagined, in part because I knew the lengths to which the Cuban authorities had gone to avoid any action that might provoke a military response from the United States and its terrible consequences. The idea that Cuba would elaborate a plan to confront those planes on international waters was to me –and still is- absurd and irrational.

N. I would have explained that there was no reasonable basis to believe that either Roque or Castor had the possibility of flying with BTTR that weekend. Roque could not have flown with BTTR that week-end as he would have already been on his way back to Cuba by then, while Castor had not flown with BTTR in over a year, and was no longer listed as a BTTR pilot.

O. In any event, I would have provided the jury with the facts that would have contradicted the prosecutor's argument that I somehow signalled Havana that neither one would be flying and that this action enabled the shoot down to occur. At a severed trial on Count III, I would have testified that I had never written or communicated in any manner that Roque and Castor would not be flying that weekend, or that they had been warned not to.

P. Operation Venecia was a major effort by the Directorate of Intelligence to denounce the BTTR organization both domestically and internationally for their unlawful violations of Cuban sovereignty with the intention of bringing about a halt to their continuing violation of Cuban airspace. Had I been able to testify, I would have explained that that project involved much more than the mere return of an agent (Roque) to Cuba, as portrayed at trial.

My assignment to work in

with Toni Woodley, one of the leaders of the Unite the Union in UK

Humor from my Pen

with Graciela Ramirez, leader of the Free the Five International Committee

extricating him from Miami was complicated. Roque was a Cuban MIG pilot who defected from Cuba to the United States. He was immediately acclaimed as a hero in Miami. A book he wrote about his exploits was published by the Cuban American National Foundation and distributed widely. He was sought after by community groups and organizations in Miami as a speaker.

He was therefore a public figure. He was also a married man whose disappearance would be noticed immediately. Moreover, we suspected he might have already come under counter-intelligence surveillance. Working with him, meeting him and arranging his return, exposed me and others to detection. Extricating him from Miami and returning him to Cuba demanded a considerable effort, requiring me to focus my attention and resources to the utmost in order to assure his successful departure and travel through a third country. I was also given risky last minute assignments, such as video-recording him leaving the CANF offices in Miami.

Q. Roque's return to Cuba and press conference achieved significant results. He released the names and phone numbers of the FBI agents he encountered, as well as photographs and other materials that demonstrated his deep involvement in the Miami community and civic organizations. But most important were his revelations regarding the criminal nature of the BTTR and its plans to carry out terrorist activities against the Cuban people. These revelations were, of course, overshadowed by the tragic events of February 24.

AA. The intercepted high frequency messages, introduced at trial, revealed that I was recognized and received special commendation from headquarters for my work on Operation Venecia, an operation which was considered successful and received special attention from the Commander in Chief who met twice with Roque. At no time was I given such commendation for Operation Escorpion.

BB. Much was made of my having responded to the commendation by referring to our work as having "ended successfully" which was interpreted as if I was writing about the shoot down rather than Operation Venecia. Nothing could be further from the truth. As I mentioned, it is very clear from the specific wording and context that I was being recognized for my work in

Operation Venecia.

CC. I also wanted to testify to correct the misinterpretation of the language in that commendation that spoke of my work in dealing with the "provocations carried out by the government of the United States this past February 24 ," as if that was a reference to the alleged plan to shoot down BTTR aircrafts. In fact, it was a reference to my efforts in the aftermath of the shoot down to determine on that day, and for a few days thereafter, whether the public clamour in Miami for a possible attack on Cuba, as well as the provocative public statements from some within the U.S. Government, signalled a real threat against my country

DD. Immediately after the events of February 24, I worked for several days, practically without sleep, collecting information, monitoring TV, listening to the radio and reading many newspapers. Fortunately, the United States did not respond militarily, but I was recognized for having helped determine if a potentially dangerous situation was unfolding.

EE. Finally, the government distorted the reasons for my promotion to Captain on June 6th. 1996, arguing that my alleged work on the shoot down earned me my promotion. Had I been able to testify, I could have explained that in fact, by that time, I had been in grade as a lieutenant for four years, and was promoted on the anniversary date of the founding of the Ministry of the Interior, together with all other lieutenants who had served for four years without blemish, including Nilo Hernandez, a co-defendant who had nothing to do with Escorpion but who had also served four years. In Cuba it is the period of service that qualifies one for promotion and I received my promotion on that basis alone.

I recognize that testifying at trial would mean also submitting myself to cross examination. Given my innocence of the charges in Count III, I would have been entirely willing to do so at a separate trial on those charges.

I came to Florida in service to my country, unarmed, to contribute to end violence against my people and therefore to save lives. That I would be charged with a conspiracy to murder was the furthest thing from my thinking and reality. It is my hope that this writing assists the Court in its efforts to find the truth and restore justice.

Pursuant to the oath requirements of 28 U.S.C. § 1746, I have made the above affidavit, swearing to its truth under penalties of perjury this 16th day of March, 2011.

Gerardo Hernández

with Marc Vandepitte and Katrien Demuynck, leaders of the Free the Five Committee in Belgium

EPILOGUE
by Gilbert Brownstone

Political satire in cartoons and caricatures has been around for centuries. They can be traced as far back as the Protestant Reformation in 1517 and Martin Luther's attacks against the Catholic Church. The first example of them in North America is Benjamin Franklin's drawing "join or die" done in 1754. Ever since then political cartoons have played an important role in forming public opinion in the United States. This is due in large part to their simplicity and directness. They reach a much larger audience than editorials and have thus played an important role in awakening awareness and consciousness.

Most unfortunately this has not been the case for the drawings of Gerardo Hernández. Gerardo's works have nothing to do with political satire. Instead they more importantly denounce injustice. His cartoons depict not only injustice to himself, and the other members of the Cuban Five, but also show the injustice and double standards of the government of the United States and in particular its judicial system. Over the 15 years of their incarceration no major media in the United States has dared to raise the issue of the injustice done to Gerardo and the Cuban Five and thus his works have been silenced. This is also true for the other four: Ramón Labanino, Antonio Guerrero, Fernando González, and René González. This is the reason why this compilation of Gerardo's cartoons is so important. This book will give us the opportunity to reach more people who unfortunately have previously never heard about the Cuban Five and the great injustice being perpetrated against them.

Since the Cuban revolution of 1959 the United States has used every conceivable means at their disposal to overthrow the Cuban regime. Since the Bay of Pigs fiasco in 1962 the U.S. government has left this task to the rogue elements of the Cuban exile community in Miami who make up only a small fraction of the 800 thousand Cubans who live in Southern Florida. Known as the Cuban Mafia, they are well financed and are extremely dangerous and will stop at nothing in implementing their plans to destabilize Cuban society with their final goal being the overthrow of the Cuban government.

In the 1990s the Cuban Mafia became even more murderous by committing bombings in Havana. All this happened with the knowledge and complicity of the CIA and the U.S. government. Despite the repeated appeals of Cuba to the U.S. government to stop these terrorist activities the attacks continued unabated. Cuba was in a position where it had no other recourse to protect its citizens and homeland than to send a small group of intelligence agents, including the Cuban Five, to monitor the activities of the Cuban mafia and report back to Havana. The assignment of the Cuban Five was not to spy on the U.S. or its military but to uncover the cowardly plans of these exile groups. The Cuban government even went so far as to provide the U.S. government with all the information the Cuban Five had collected. The FBI turned around and instead of arresting the real terrorists arrested the anti terrorist Cuban Five group.

The trial began in November 2000 and was held in Miami, the only city in the U.S. where agents of the Cuban government could not receive a fair trial. Because there was no evidence that the Cuban Five had spied on the U.S. government they were convicted of trumped up conspiracy charges. The other four received lesser sentences, including Ramón who now has a 30 year sentence, Antonio whose sentence is 21 years and 10 months and Fernando who was released in February 2014, is now back home in Cuba with his family, as is René, who returned after serving his full 15 year sentence. But Gerardo, because he was the leader of the group, he is now in the maximum security penitentiary in Victorville California condemned to two life sentences and fifteen years, as though one term were not enough. You may ask what kind of heinous crime could he have committed to receive this draconian sentence. Did he kill anybody? No, he and the others came unarmed. All Gerardo ever did was to try and protect his people and his country armed only with his sense of justice, his spirit of resistance and his moral values. All of these attributes can be seen in his drawings reproduced in this book. They depict the complicity and the contradictions that the U.S. has with the Miami terrorists, with a perfect mixture of humor, irony and sharp wit. On several occasions I have had the privilege of visiting Gerardo Hernández. Over my lifetime I have met and talked with some very influential and remarkable people, but to this day I have never met anyone as inspiring, stimulating, passionate and compassionate as Gerardo. On top of that I have to add humorous. After every one of these visits, which can last up to five hours, Gerardo has made me feel so good as though I was the man who came to get his support and comfort rather than him. As we hug and say goodbye on these visits I am already thinking about when I can come back after having spent the most wonderful and exhilarating moments of my life.

Gilbert Brownstone

Gilbert Brownstone, - American reviewer, museum expert, art collector and curator. President of the "Brownstone Art Foundation."

Editorial Letra Viva
2014
251 Valencia Avenue, #253
Coral Gables, FL 33114, USA

www.ingramcontent.com/pod-product-compliance
Lightning Source LLC
Chambersburg PA
CBHW041546220426
43665CB00002B/49